Weather Poems

Compiled by John Foster

Contents

Acknowledgements

The Editor and Publisher wish to thank the following who have kindly given permission for the use of copyright material:

Gina Douthwaite for 'Clouds' © 1993 Gina Douthwaite; Eric Finney for 'Out in all weathers' and 'Wind and Sun' both © 1993 Eric Finney; John Foster for 'On sunny days' © 1993 John Foster; Jenny Morris for 'Weather at work' © 1993 Jenny Morris; Judith Nicholls for 'Shadows' © 1993 Judith Nicholls; Jack Ousbey for 'Snow' © 1993 Jack Ousbey.

Weather at work

I'm a speeding hailstone,
An icy lump.

I'm a clap of thunder,
A noisy thump.

I'm a chilly snowflake,
soft and white.

2

I'm a ray of sunshine,
warm and bright.

I'm a falling raindrop,
sploshing to the ground.

I'm a winter snowball,
hard and round.

3

I'm a flash of lightning,
A magic sight.

You can see me zigzag,
Lighting up the night.

Jenny Morris

Wind and sun

'Let's see who's stronger,'
Said Wind to Sun.
'That boy down there
With the brown coat on:
Let's see who can make him
Take off his coat first.'
They agreed on the test
And Wind blew till he burst.

Then Wind blew some more,
In his rage made a storm.
But the boy just hugged
His coat tight to keep warm.

6

So Wind gave up—
He knew he had failed,
And now out from the clouds
The blazing Sun sailed.
The boy opened his coat
Saying, 'Wow, this hot weather!'
And before very long
Took it off altogether.

Eric Finney

Clouds

Water in clouds
falling as rain,
water in gutters
glugging down drains,
water in streams
twists to the sea,
rises as clouds
floating free.

Gina Douthwaite

Out in all weathers

It snowed in the night
And the whole world is white.
I'm off out with my friends
For a mighty snow fight.

It's windy today
And the trees swing and sway;
See the wind take my kite
Up, up, up and away.

Today it's all rain—
It's really a pain.
I could just stay in
And watch telly again.
But maybe not yet:
Instead I'll just get
My wellies and things—
And go out and get wet.

Eric Finney

Snow

Soft snow has fallen
During the night,
The grass snuggles under
A carpet of white.

We climb in our wellies
Then button up warm,
Make footsteps in circles
Around the white lawn.

We roll up the snow,
Make snow-bricks to stack
And build a white giant,
A snowman called Jack.

When I look through my window
Much later at night,
Jack is just standing
Silent and white.

Jack Ousbey

13

On sunny days

On sunny days
I dash outside,
To swing on the swing
And slide on the slide.

I bounce my ball
On the wall of the school.
I play in the sand
And splash in the pool.

Then, tired and thirsty,
I sit in the shade,
To eat an ice-cream
And drink cold lemonade.

John Foster

Shadows

Stand with your back
to the shining sun,
watch your shadow
dance and run.

Stand and face
the shining sun,
look ahead —
your shadow's gone!

Judith Nicholls

16